# the swimming dragon

# *the swimming dragon*

A Chinese Way to
## Fitness, Beautiful Skin,
## Weight Loss & High Energy

# T. K. Shih

Edited by Charles Stein

Station Hill Press

Published by Station Hill Press, Inc., Barrytown, New York 12507.


Produced by the Institute for Publishing Arts, Barrytown, New York 12507, a not-for-profit, tax-exempt organization.

Cover designed by Susan Quasha.
Text designed by Susan Quasha and Charles Stein.
Photography by Douglas Baz.

**Library of Congress Cataloging-in-Publication Data**

Shih, T. K. (Tzu Kuo)
    The swimming dragon : a Chinese way to fitness, beautiful skin, weight loss, and high energy / T. K. Shih.
      p. cm.
    ISBN 0-88268-063-3
    1. Ch'i kung. I. Title.
RA781.8.S55 1988                    89-4053
613.7—dc19                         CIP

## AUTHOR'S ACKNOWLEDGEMENTS

    This book arises in response to many requests from my students, whose enthusiasm for, and success with, the Swimming Dragon has demonstrated its special appropriateness for Westerners. Since the book derives from a text that I wrote in Chinese, I am indebted to Charles Stein for creating an English version that meets the needs of readers here. This version necessarily goes beyond the scope of the original. The original translation from Chinese was done by Charles Shih, my brother, under the expert guidance of Dr. De-Ying Huang, my wife, a master of the Swimming Dragon in her own right; Bill Brown and Melanie Shih, also assisted these efforts. Daniel Bauch some time ago helped me with a short English description of the exercise suitable for use in classes. Van Witcher worked on an early version of the text, and Carol Dowd and Barbara Leon, along with the publishers, read the text and made valuable suggestions. Douglas Baz made the photographs. Susan Quasha, working with Charles Stein, designed the book. George Quasha initiated and directed the project.
    To all who have assisted I am deeply grateful, and it is my hope that this exercise will bring health and well-being to many people.

Manufactured in the United States of America.

# Contents

# *Introduction*

The Swimming Dragon is an ancient Chinese exercise that comes to us through the Taoist tradition. If practiced diligently and regularly, the Swimming Dragon has the power to improve our health, enhance our physical appearance, and promote our general well-being. It is especially celebrated for its ability to improve skin tone and control weight without dieting, but the main purpose of the Swimming Dragon is to increase the production of the vital energy known as "ch'i" and to enhance its circulation throughout the body. The circulation of ch'i in the body is a deeply satisfying and pleasurable experience; therefore, while many "exercises," however beneficial, are often a chore, Swimming Dragon is uniquely enjoyable to perform.

The Swimming Dragon is a self-contained exercise that is generally practiced by repeating a short cycle of movements in sessions lasting from five to twenty minutes. Each repeated cycle of the exercise takes about one minute. It is easy to learn and perform and brings pleasant and beneficial results as soon as one begins to practice it. Of course, it is advantageous to study Swimming Dragon through the teachings of a qualified instructor; nevertheless, the instructions in this book are all you need to learn the exercise and experience its benefits.

The ch'i energy that we experience during Swimming Dragon comes from two sources: the air we breathe and the food we eat. It is generated from air and food by means of the specific Swimming Dragon exercises. Once the ch'i is created, it can be used to sustain health and vitality if it is properly stored in our body. Because ch'i comes from air and food and is developed by exercise, and stored by the body, the practice of Swimming Dragon is divided into three phases that successively make use of these three facts. There is first a preparatory exercise called "Soaring Dragon Feeds on Ch'i" that emphasizes a special breathing process; second, the Swimming Dragon exercise itself; and finally, a period of sitting meditation called "Sitting Dragon" where the energy generated during the previous two exercises can be stored in a special bodily area called the "lower tan-t'ien."

In this book, the instructions for Soaring Dragon Feeds on Ch'i precede the instructions for the Swimming Dragon exercise, and instructions for Sitting Dragon follow. The book also contains an appendix including two additional Taoist practices: a meditation for relaxing muscles, nerves, and organs, as well as instructions for a standing meditation.

Though the Swimming Dragon is a complete exercise in itself and can be practiced without the preliminary or follow-up exercises, its benefits can be increased by performing it with them.

## How to Use This Book

The basic instruction in this book is the Swimming Dragon Exercise itself. Therefore the best way to begin is with the Swimming Dragon. Learn it well, and then later add the preliminary exercise. The instructions for Swimming Dragon may seem detailed and, at first glance, a little bit complicated. The movements, however, are essentially simple once you understand them. Take your time in learning the movements. It is a good idea not to try to learn the whole form at once. Don't overextend yourself. Take as many breaks as you need in order to make learning Swimming Dragon easy and enjoyable. It may be helpful to have a friend read the instructions out loud while you are learning the form. And always keep in mind that the essence of this practice is relaxation and free-flowing effortlessness.

Once you have gotten the exercise under control so that you can perform it without referring to the instructions, give yourself a few days to practice only the form. Then go back and check the instructions to see if you have left anything out. The significance of certain aspects of the form may only become clear to you as your practice improves. It is therefore a good idea to read through the instructions every so often in order to take note of refinements you may have missed when first learning them. Remember that you don't have to learn everything all at once. Give yourself time to absorb the movements slowly and naturally.

Once you are comfortable with the Swimming Dragon, you can add the Soaring Dragon Feeds on Ch'i, Sitting Dragon, and the appended meditation practices.

## Swimming Dragon and Ch'i Kung

The Swimming Dragon, Soaring Dragon Feeds on Ch'i, Sitting Dragon, Relaxation Meditation, and Standing Meditation all belong to the very large family of Chinese exercises known as "ch'i kung." These exercises generally are designed to cultivate, circulate and store vital energy, promote longevity, and improve health. The word "ch'i" means vital energy—the energy that animates both mind and body. The word "kung" means exercise as well as time spent in performing exercises successfully.

The concept of "ch'i" is a very interesting topic. (The word is often spelled "qi" or given its Japanese form "ki.") To persons who have not practiced some form of ch'i kung, ch'i seems to be some sort of mystical substance whose very existence is open to doubt. But it does not take very much practice at an exercise such as the Swimming Dragon before the ch'i begins to show itself in the form of very definite experiences. Though these experiences differ for different people, after a while you will become familiar with what they are in your case. At that point you will understand why the production and internal circulation of ch'i is treasured by Chinese medical tradition as the very essence of healthful practice.

## Ch'i Kung and Chinese Medicine

Ch'i kung practices are based on ancient principles of Chinese medicine. This system is an extraordinarily so-phisticated system for maintaining the good health of those who are healthy and curing those who are ill. It is concerned not only with preventing and curing disease, but also with increasing general vitality and well-being. It is not necessary to know anything about the intricacies of Chinese medicine in order to experience its benefits, but it can be helpful, when practicing the Swimming Dragon or other ch'i kung exercises, to understand some of its basic principles. As a practitioner of Chinese medi-cine for more than forty years, it is my opinion that the most effective way of gaining and maintaining health and vitality is by cultivating ch'i energy by practicing ch'i kung. Therefore I wish to write a few words about the principles of Chinese medicine on which ch'i kung is based.

## Chinese Medicine

Chinese medicine is based on the idea that a living being is an ENERGY SYSTEM. All life is based on ch'i. There are many different kinds of energy or ch'i in the universe and many special forms of ch'i that flow through our bodies and keep them alive. These different kinds of energy are connected to our bodily organs and flow in a system of channels called "meridians" and "collaterals " (*figure 1*). The system of the twelve meridians and eight collaterals and the differentiation of ch'i energy into yin and yang phases form the basis of Chinese medicine and all ch'i kung or energy exercises, including the Swimming Dragon.

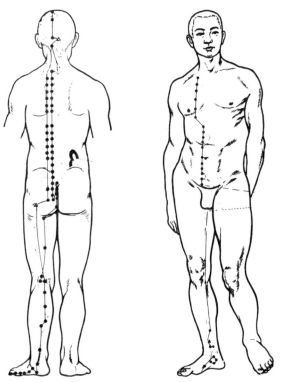

*figure 1*                    **acupuncture meridians**

Each meridian is associated with one of the main bodily organs. The name of each organ, as understood in Chinese medicine, refers not only to the physical organ given by the name (heart, lung, liver, large intestine, etc.), but to the whole system of energy and energy flow that derives from that organ. Each organ has its characteristic energy or ch'i, and it is this energy that flows through the meridians.

The meridians pass through the arms, legs, body and trunk and connect with their associated organs. Six meridians flow through the arms and six through the legs. Along the meridians are the acupuncture points. These are precise locations that can be used to regulate the functioning of the organ/meridian systems. The meridians can be stimulated or sedated by massaging the acupuncture points, by the application of heat or needles to these points, and most importantly, through ch'i kung practices.

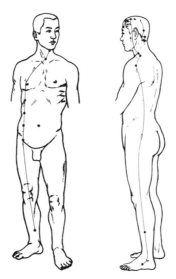

## Yin and Yang

Ch'i energy manifests in two forms: yin and yang. Everything in nature is in a process of orderly change. Everything that changes—everything that grows, decays, or is in motion—involves the flow and balance of yin and yang as complementary forms of energy. All phenomena, including the things that happen within our bodies, involve both yin and yang. Yang ch'i is warm and active energy, while yin ch'i is cool and receptive. The health of the organs depends upon the flow of ch'i and upon the proper balance of yin and yang within each organ/ meridian system. When the flow of ch'i along a meridian is obstructed or when the balance of yin and yang within an organ is upset, illness occurs. The Swimming Dragon and other ch'i kung exercises help both to maintain the flow of vital energy and to maintain proper yin/yang balance within the organs.

*figure 2*

## Vitality and the Abundance of Ch'i

Our sense of vitality—our youthfulness, agility, vigor, and general health—does not only depend upon the flow and balance of ch'i, but upon the abundance of it as well. Ch'i kung practice is therefore also concerned with increasing the quantity of ch'i energy and storing it in the channels called "collaterals" and in the three storage vessels known as "tan-t'iens " (*figure 3*).

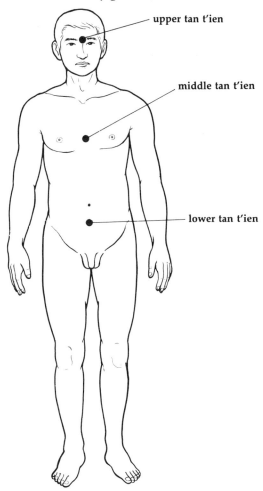

upper tan t'ien

middle tan t'ien

lower tan t'ien

*figure 3*

The collaterals are eight channels that store energy. The three tan-t'iens are areas within the body that are connected with energy. The tan-t'iens are located in the centers of the head, chest, and abdomen. As one's practice improves over time, the collaterals and tan-t'iens become full. The energy found there becomes available, whenever needed, to supplement energy in the meridian/organ systems.

Though "ch'i" is the general term for energy, when it is found in the three tan-t'iens it takes three different forms: it is called "ching" when in the lower tan-t'ien; it is called "ch'i" when in the middle tan-t'ien; and "shen" when in the upper tan-t'ien. Ching is a strong form of energy associated with sexual energy and capable of manifesting externally as sperm and sexual fluids. Ch'i proper does not manifest in any external, material form, but is experienced as it circulates through the body. Shen, like ch'i, cannot be perceived externally, but is experienced subjectively as a feeling of clarity and alertness. These three forms of energy are capable of being transformed into one another: ching becomes ch'i and ch'i becomes shen. But shen also can become ch'i, and ch'i, once generated and in circulation, can be stored in the lower tan-t'ien as ching.

## Ch'i Kung and Modern Science

Though ch'i kung is taught using terms from traditional Chinese medicine and Taoist mythology, the effects of ch'i kung practices are presently undergoing careful study by modern medical researchers world-wide, particularly in China, but increasingly in the United States as well. In 1985, The Ch'i Kung Scientific Research Society of China was established in Beijing under the sponsorship of the Chinese Government to develop and expand scientific study of ch'i kung. I myself was privileged to be one of the founders of this society and am presently serving as a senior consultant to it. It is my conviction that the effects of ch'i kung practice can be documented and understood by scientific means.

## Special Features of the Swimming Dragon Exercise

During the Swimming Dragon exercise, the body smoothly and evenly rises and lowers and, at the same time, swings to the left and right. In Chinese mythology, the images of dragons are frequently used to represent the action of internal bodily energy. In this exercise, therefore, the risings of the body are said to be like a "flying dragon ascending to the clouds," and the lowerings are said to be like "a coiling dragon entering the sea."

*figure 4*

14

The movements are simple and beautiful, and the swinging movements fully stretch out the body. The Swimming Dragon exercise requires that the entire body, especially the waist and abdominal area, perform large scale swinging movements. These movements open capillaries in the muscles that are normally closed. This opening, in turn, increases the flow of energy, blood, and the supply of oxygen. The increased blood flow, together with increased hormonal activity, causes the fat of the waist, abdomen, shoulders, neck, back, buttocks, and thighs to be transformed and reduced.

After practicing this exercise, the functioning of the intestines and stomach is improved, and, even though the appetite and possibly the consumption of food and drink may increase, the waistline is reduced. This exercise thus allows one to lose weight in a relaxed and pleasant way without having to excessively reduce food intake. After doing this exercise, people generally feel that their waist and kidneys are strong, that their lower abdomen is warm, and that they are full of energy. After long term practice (one year) people have feelings of a "springtime" appearance and are much more healthy and attractive.

One of the special features of the Swimming Dragon exercise is that moving the body from side to side with legs together while shifting the pelvis stimulates the groin area. This in turn stimulates the endocrine system. This system then moves toward dynamic rebalancing and self regulation. The resulting internal secretions act on each organ of the body. The facial skin relaxes and becomes smoother and more beautiful. This is because hormones enable slack, atrophied facial muscles to recover elasticity; they act upon the skin to increase the elasticity of the subcutaneous tissues. Regulation of the endocrine system also has beneficial effects for those who are overweight.

The Swimming Dragon should be practiced with a fundamentally relaxed attitude. While you are learning the movements of Swimming Dragon, it is natural that you may have a tendency to tense up a bit as your body learns unfamiliar positions and movements. It is important to gradually recognize these tensions in your body and release them as best you can. As you perform the movement, allow your attention to scan your body for "tense" areas, and simply let go of the tension as much as you are able to. As time goes on, you will find that you are able to release more and more of your muscular tension. Eventually you will be able to perform the whole Swimming Dragon as a single smooth and sensuous movement without any tension or strain.

A particular area that should be kept relaxed at all times is the lower tan-t'ien (*see page 11*). Energy can only collect in the tan-t'ien if the whole lower belly is relaxed. Relaxing the lower belly can be accomplished by relaxing the waist and the lower back and by breathing in the lower belly.

The Swimming Dragon is a beautiful form, and it should be delightful and enjoyable to perform. Let it be a pleasure!

## Time of Practice

The Swimming Dragon exercise should be performed for twenty minutes each day. Since each cycle takes one minute, this means that the exercise is performed twenty times. It is best if these twenty cycles are performed in a single session—the more cycles one performs, the more energy one generates. But if circumstances do not allow practicing all twenty cycles at once, they can be practiced at different times during the day as is convenient. Additional cycles can also be performed when the opportunity or desire arises. For people who work in an office, it is often rewarding to do three or four cycles of Swimming Dragon after an hour or so of desk work. The Swimming Dragon naturally realigns the spine, gets the "kinks" out of one's muscles, and recharges one's energy.

A general rule is that it is always best to practice when you want to practice and when you are able to practice without rushing. If you are truly relaxed and able to keep your mind focused on what you are doing, even one or two cycles of Swimming Dragon will be beneficial. But if you are distracted and just "putting in time" on your exercise, even a complete round of twenty cycles will be of little benefit.

At the same time regular daily practice is the only way to get the full benefit of the exercise. Even a single day without practice breaks the chain of the exercise and interrupts the gradual development of ch'i energy.

The best time to do your full round of practice is one hour or so after eating, or at least when you are not hungry. If abdominal discomfort is experienced due to practicing too soon after mealtimes, you should discontinue exercising to prevent possible harm to your stomach.

Because this exercise acts on the abdominal area, causing the internal organs to gently move, and because it can also accelerate the peristalsis of the intestines and stomach and promote the appetite, those wishing to reduce weight must also control their intake of food and drink so they do not eat more than usual (though it is not usually necessary to reduce intake).

Of course, the more you practice, the greater the benefits. If you want to lose a lot of weight or lose weight more quickly, you can do two or three twenty minute cycles daily. Three twenty minute sessions a day, every day, will actually make wrinkles disappear! Whereas there are inherent dangers in doing too much of most exercises, there is really no such thing as doing too much Swimming Dragon.

# Benefits of Practicing the Swimming Dragon

The Swimming Dragon is actually a comprehensive system of care for the internal organs and organ/meridian systems. In particular, the movements have beneficial influences on the intestines, the stomach, the lungs, and the kidneys and encourage development of what has come to be known as "the relaxation response."

### Weight Loss and Benefits to Digestive System

For many people the most enticing benefit of regular Swimming Dragon practice is its ability to help in weight loss without dieting or even reducing food-intake. But there are additional benefits for the digestive system as well. Daily practice promotes the more efficient and regular functioning of the intestines. For many people, after a short period of time, constipation is reduced or eliminated, and bowel movement becomes easy and regular. This is due to gentle internal massaging of the intestines and bowels during the exercise. When the bowels are free to flow normally, food and waste does not stagnate and putrefy. This results in an improvement in general health and also allows the body to absorb the food it needs in a normal, efficient manner. This in turn leads to a gradual normalization of body weight. At the same time, the reduction of stagnant bulk in the intestines reduces the pressure on the other internal organs, allowing them to function more efficiently.

### Benefits for Skin Tone

The stimulation of the endocrine system and the deepening of the breathing process that occur during Swimming Dragon practice have the capacity to vivify the skin, giving it tone and youthful luster. If practiced in three cycles of twenty minutes a day, Swimming Dragon causes wrinkles due to aging to simply disappear.

### Benefits for Respiratory System

Swimming Dragon also profoundly benefits the lungs and improves the entire breathing process. Each cycle of the exercise progressively releases tension in the area around the ribs and lower abdomen, allowing each breath to grow more and more profound. Deeper breathing means an increased level of oxygen in the blood, which in turn helps the whole body to function vigorously, enhances the body's resistance to infectious disease, improves brain functions, and, last but not least, contributes to the development of a healthy and robust complexion.

### Benefits for the Kidneys

The Swimming Dragon also has a profoundly beneficial effect on the group of functions associated in Chinese medicine with the kidneys: the production of ch'i, sexual functions, as well as the elimination of wastes. The kidneys are called "The Mother of Ch'i." Strong kidneys are vital to the strength of the other organs of the body. Swimming Dragon massages and stimulates the kidneys, and they in turn strengthen and nourish the other organs with the ch'i they generate.

## Benefits for Spine, Nervous System, and Meridians

When practicing the Swimming Dragon, the spine is twisted in an "S" shape and extended to its maximum length. There are acupuncture points all along the spine that are massaged because of this S-shape curving. As a result, all the organs connected to these points receive benefits. When the cervical vertebrae are moved, points associated with eyes, ears, nose, chest, heart, throat, hands, and vagus nerve are massaged. When the thoracic vertebrae are moved, points associated with the trachea, lungs, heart, hands, stomach, liver, eyes, ears, diaphragm, pericardium, spleen, gall bladder, bone, and blood are activated. When the lumbar vertebrae are moved, points associated with the large intestine, caecum, genitals, knees, feet, legs, triple warmer, womb, kidneys, adrenal glands, and prostate gland are massaged. When the sacrum and coccyx are moved, points connected with the bladder, genitals, small intestine, and anus are activated.

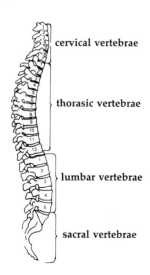

cervical vertebrae

thorasic vertebrae

lumbar vertebrae

sacral vertebrae

21

The curvilinear movement of the spine not only benefits the cervical, thoracic, and lumbar vertebrae and their associated points and organs, but it can also serve to fully regulate the du (governor) and ren (conception) meridians. When the du and ren meridians are open, the ch'i and blood throughout the entire body are vigorous and flourishing.

*figure 5*

22

### Benefits for the Middle Aged and the Elderly

The waist moves the entire body up and down in a "shake the head and wag the tail" fashion. These movements have marked effects on strengthening the ribs, making the kidneys healthy, and nourishing the brain. This movement also enables the spine to open up and lengthen.

The fat of middle aged and elderly people is generally due to the gradual decrease of sex hormone secretions and the lowering of the basic metabolism. These phenomena cause the fat in the body to congeal. When practicing the Swimming Dragon, emphasis is placed on the waist, abdomen, and buttocks. This results in greater depletion of the fat that has built up in these areas. Also, as I have mentioned, frequent and regular practice restores vitality to skin and complexion and reduces wrinkles and other effects of aging.

### Enhances Ability to Relax

Another benefit of regular practice is the improvement in one's ability to relax. Western medicine has shown that excessive excitation of the sympathetic nervous system and irritation of the adrenal cortex, which often result from the fast pace and stressful conditions of modern life, are major factors in causing high blood pressure, coronary heart disease, tachycardia (excessively rapid movement of the heart), neurasthenia (weakening of the nerves), as well as other functional disorders. Recent research in China and elsewhere points to a series of physiological effects that frequently follow practice of ch'i kung exercises such as Swimming Dragon and greatly reduce these reactions. These effects include: 1. a decrease in adrenaline secretion; 2. activation of the autonomic nervous system and de-activation of the sympathetic nervous system; 3. lowering of plasma dopamine and B-hydroxylase; 4. relaxation of the tenseness of the blood vessels; 5. increase in hydrolase metabolism levels; 6. elevation of levels of prolactin in blood plasma. These physiological effects are experienced directly as a feeling of deep relaxation and release of tension.

## *The Development of Ch'i*

As I mentioned before, though the Swimming Dragon offers all the above mentioned, specific health benefits, its main benefit is the production and circulation of ch'i itself. Balanced circulation of abundant ch'i leads to long life and energetic vitality.

# *Method of Practice*

The Swimming Dragon Exercise has three parts:

1. A Preliminary Practice called "Soaring Dragon Feeds on Ch'i"
2. The Swimming Dragon Form
3. Sitting Dragon Meditation Practice

## 1: SOARING DRAGON FEEDS ON CH'I

The Soaring Dragon Feeds on Ch'i is a series of movements to prepare for performing Swimming Dragon. If you regularly perform ten or twenty rounds of Swimming Dragon in the morning, it is a good idea to do Soaring Dragon as a setting up exercise. For more casual performance of Swimming Dragon, however, Soaring Dragon is not necessary.

The name of this exercise comes from the fact that the air we breathe is a primary source for ch'i energy. This exercise emphasizes breathing with movement. Metaphorically, the Swimming Dragon (ourselves as performers of this exercise) "feed" on ch'i by breathing as we prepare to "swim."

## *To perform Soaring Dragon Feeds on Ch'i:*

Stand naturally erect with feet spread apart as wide as your shoulders. Let your arms hang down on both sides of your body. Breathe slowly. Relax your entire body. Let your eyes look within, keeping your spirit peaceful and serene. Your mind should focus on the springtime of youth so that a smile naturally appears on your face.

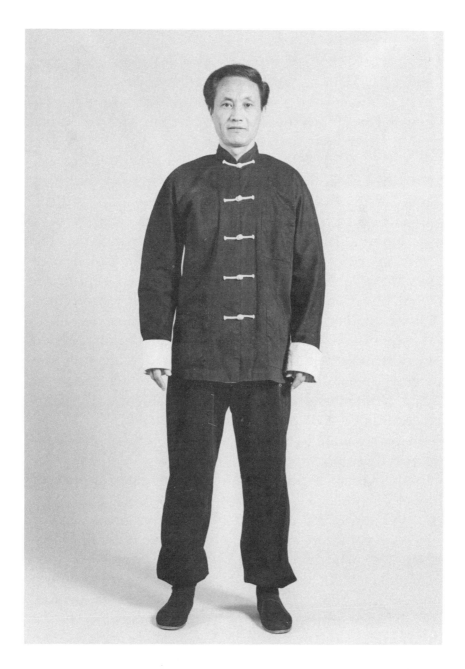

*figure 6*

27

Now raise your two hands outward from your sides and upward in an arc shape until they are above your head. Let your two palms come together and the fingers of each hand touch the corresponding fingers on the other hand. Draw your heels together (bring your left heel to your right heel) and let your toes point slightly outward. Now raise your heels (standing on the front of your feet) and inhale deeply. Gently contract your anus and the area in your back above your waist where your kidneys are located. Think of your energy as moving from the lower part of your trunk upward along the du meridian (*see page 121*). Now slowly bring your joined palms down along the front of your body while at the same time slowly sinking your heels to the ground and exhaling. As you exhale, guide the ch'i energy down along the ren meridian (*see page 121*) with your joined palms until the energy comes to settle in the lower tan-t'ien. Then let your two palms separate and move slowly to the sides of your body. Continue breathing naturally.

Separate your two feet to shoulder width. Relax your entire body. Breathe slowly, once again allowing your spirit to become peaceful and serene. Enter a state of inner quietude.

While breathing for the following movements, inhale through your nose and exhale through your mouth. Place your feet a bit wider than shoulder width. Relax your shoulders and "sit down" as if you were straddling a horse. Now allow your waist to bend and lean backwards. At the same time, raise your hands in front of you until they are level with the ground and inhale deeply. Then bend the waist and lean forward, lower your hands in an arc downward, and exhale.

Next, take a deep breath and while you are inhaling, shrug your shoulders, lift your heels, and contract your anus and the areas around your kidneys. Continue inhaling and allow your head to rise up on your neck slightly, slowly stretching your neck, expanding your chest, and naturally swelling your lower abdomen. When you feel that you have inhaled sufficiently (without completely filling your lungs), roll your shoulders in a circle towards the rear and continue to inhale. Next, slowly exhale; at the same time slowly lower your heels. Also, at the same time, bend your knees gradually, and let your body lean forward, contracting your lower abdomen slightly. Lower your hands naturally in front of your body so that as much of the used air as possible is expelled as you exhale.

"Soaring Dragon Feeds on Ch'i" employs normal abdominal breathing accompanied by a relaxing of the shoulders. The entire body is relaxed. The large movements of the muscles around the ribs and those of the diaphragm not only make it possible to more fully absorb fresh air (Taoists call this "living ch'i") but also to be able to more fully eliminate carbon dioxide (Taoists call this "dead ch'i"). Moreover, with persistent practice, there will be a marked increase in the vital capacity of the lungs. In this way, one can breathe in more fresh air so that the supply of oxygen to the muscles will be ample and the amount of dead ch'i retained in the body will be diminished. The cells of each tissue will be enlivened, and the metabolism will be vigorous. This will naturally promote a healthy and beautiful body.

# Practice Principles

- Don't overextend yourself. Take as many breaks as you need in order to make learning Swimming Dragon easy and enjoyable.

- Give yourself time to absorb the movements slowly and naturally.

- Chinese medicine is based on the idea that a living being is an ENERGY SYSTEM. When the flow of ch'i along a meridian is obstructed or when the balance of yin and yang within an organ is upset, illness occurs.

- Assume a relaxed but alert attitude.

- As you perform each movement, allow your attention to scan your body for "tense" areas, and simply let go of the tension as much as you are able to.

- Relax your stomach and let your breathing come from the belly.

- Feel that your spine is very long! Allow it to stretch and expand. Imagine that your body is being suspended from the sky by a thread attached to the center of your head.

- Your head should feel suspended from the pai-hui point, floating upward as if on its own.

- As you move, maintain your weight equally on both feet.

- Your body weight should be released downward.

# 2: SWIMMING DRAGON EXERCISE

## *Overview*

In the Swimming Dragon, your hands, joined together palm to palm, move in circular orbits along the front of the body, making three circles (*see figure 7*). The arms circle around your head, then circle downward as your body progressively sinks down. Then the arms rise up as the body progressively returns to a full standing posi-

*figure 7*

tion. As your arms and body go down and come back up, the waist swings to the left and the right so that your entire spine and inner organs are in constant motion. When your hands have made a final pass by and around your head, you then stand on your toes and go into a full stretch. Your hands then return to a position in front of your lower abdomen where the palms face inward. Each cycle of the exercise is completed with a brief meditation to store energy in the lower tan-t'ien while your breathing deepens and becomes regular.

While learning Swimming Dragon and for the first month of regular practice, your breathing should be natural. Do not pay any particular attention to it, except to allow it to become regular between cycles. After you have mastered the form, you can add the special breathing pattern found under the heading "Advanced Breathing" in the "Additional Pointers" section of this book.

### Getting Started

To begin the Swimming Dragon, stand erect with your feet parallel and together and with your ankles almost touching. Your knees should be unlocked.

Allow a smile to appear on your face and bring to mind the blossoming of youth or other pleasant, happy thoughts (*See "Additional Pointers," page 100*).

Tuck in your chin slightly.

Hold your fingers together with your palms facing the sides of your body.

Center your weight over the kidney points in your feet (*see figure and description page 106*). This is done by shifting your center of gravity gently forward and back until you feel equal weight on the front (ball) and back (heel) of both feet. Remember to relax the feet so that eventually you feel your weight going into the soft area behind the ball of the foot. (This area is to the foot as the palm is to the hand.)

Feel that your spine is very long! Allow it to stretch and expand. Imagine that your body is being suspended from the sky by a thread attached to the center of your head (*see page 103*).

Bring your attention to your lower tan-t'ien (*see page 11*).

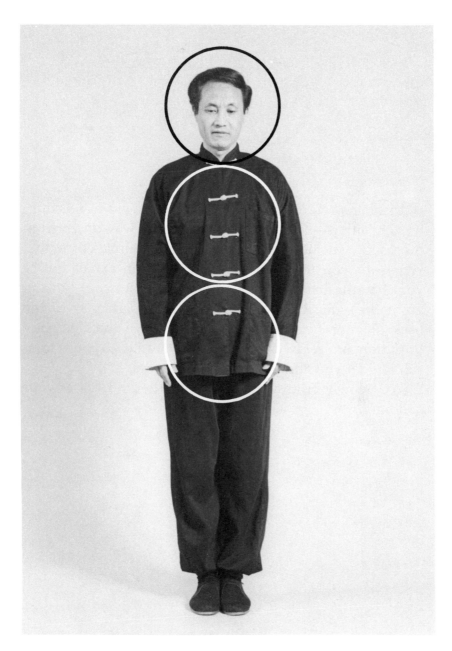

*figure 8*

Assume a relaxed but alert attitude. To aid in relaxing, let your mind—your attention—work its way down from the head, sensing any tension in your muscles or joints. Wherever you feel tension, relax with an exhalation of your breath. Just let your breath out and let your tension go at the same time. Pay attention in particular to the back of your neck and shoulders. Move them slightly until they are relaxed and comfortable. Relax your stomach and let your breathing come from the belly.

Now slowly bring your hands together in front of your abdomen.

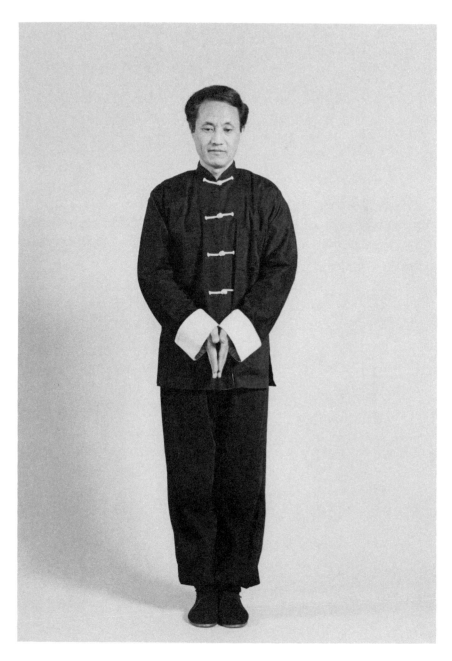

*figure 9*

Now rotate your hands, palm to palm, outward and upward, until all your fingers point upward. Your palms are together as if in prayer, your thumbs against your body.

*figure 10*

39

Your hands now begin to move slowly upward until the tips of your fingers are just below your chin.

*figure 11*

41

Continue moving your hands slowly, bending them to your left as you tilt your head slightly to the left. It is as if you were laying your head down on the back of your right hand, though your head should not actually make contact with it. Notice in figure 12 that not only the head, but the entire upper body, is tilted to the left and that the hips have begun to swing to the right.

*figure 12*

43

Your hands continue to move to the left, following your finger tips forward, your arms extending more and more.

*figure 13*

45

*figure 14*

*figure 15*

47

This movement describes a semicircle in front of your head. As your arms swing to your left and in front of you, your hips swing to the right and towards the back. As your hands come to the position straight in front of you, your hips, back, and legs are once again vertically straight up and down.

As you make this movement, allow your head to roll forward, face down, so that, when your arms are extended to the maximum in front of your head, your hands are passing in front of the crown of your head, pai-hui point (*see page 103*). Your waist is bent forward slightly.

As you move, maintain your weight equally on both feet. The weight of your arms, head, and shoulders as you lean to the left is balanced by the weight of your hips swinging out to the right. As your hips swing to the back, try not to let your buttocks stick out.

*figure 16*

Now facing the ground, you are bending your shoulders forward, counterbalanced by your hips.

Now pass your arms around towards the right side, rolling your head to the right, your hips to the left, and allowing your spine to tilt to the right. As your hips rotate, they continue to counterbalance the weight of your arms and shoulders.

Your arms should now be extended to the right. Your left hand is on top of your right, palm to palm.

*figure 17*

Keeping your hands together, turn them over on themselves so that the ends of your fingers point to the left under your chin, with your right elbow extended to the right and your right forearm parallel to the ground. As your hands turn over, you turn your head slightly to the left.

*figure 18*

53

Notice in figure 19 how the "S" curve of the spine has begun to appear.

*figure 19*

55

Now move your hands slowly to the left, keeping them together, following your finger tips until they are under your chin. As you do this, gently bend your knees slightly so that your center of gravity begins to become lower. As you perform the above movement, your spine returns to a straight up and down position, and your head returns to upright with the chin slightly tucked in.

*figure 20*

57

Your hands now continue on their path to the left. At the same time, gently shift your hips to the right and turn your head from the left to the right.

Your hands now turn over so that your left palm is pressing on top of the right, with the outer sides of your thumbs now facing forwards.

*figure 21*

Notice how the "S" curve of the spine has reappeared.

*figure 22*

61

Now let your hands move downward, making a semi-circle along the left side of your body until your wrists are against your solar plexus.

*figure* 23

63

As your hands move downward, your left palm is pressing on your right palm, and your finger tips are pointing downward. Your hands now continue to follow a circular path orbiting toward the right side. At the same time roll your hips towards the left side with your head also turning to the left. Bend your knees further so that your center of gravity shifts even lower. As your hands move to the right, they turn over so that the right palm is now pressing the left.

*figure 24*

Next, continue moving your hands down along the right side in a downward semicircle until they pass in front of your groin, the back of your left hand brushing your groin slightly. Your right hand is on top and the left hand underneath, still palm to palm. Your knees are now deeply bent.

*figure 25*

67

Your hips should be precisely over your feet. Your head turns forward as your hands pass in front of your groin.

Your center of gravity is now at its lowest point, and your body is in a half-squat position, as low as you can comfortably go.

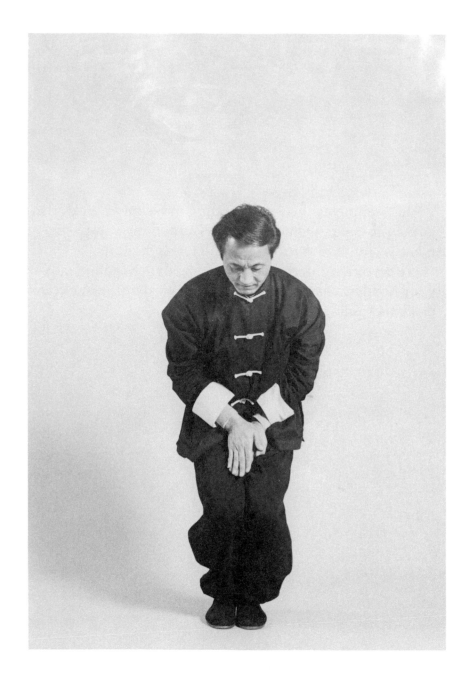

*figure 26*

This completes the top-to-bottom movement. Next, the bottom-to-top movement begins. The bottom-to-top movement is simply the reverse of the top-to-bottom.

With your right palm pressing your left palm, move your hands towards the left and upwards, turning your head and rolling your hips to the right.

*figure 27*

Move your hands upward along the left side of your body until they reach the level of your solar plexus. As your hands move upward along the left, your hips swing to the right, your head faces to the right, and you begin to straighten your knees, raising your center of gravity.

*figure 28*

Continue moving your hands until they are in front of your solar plexus, left palm pressing right.

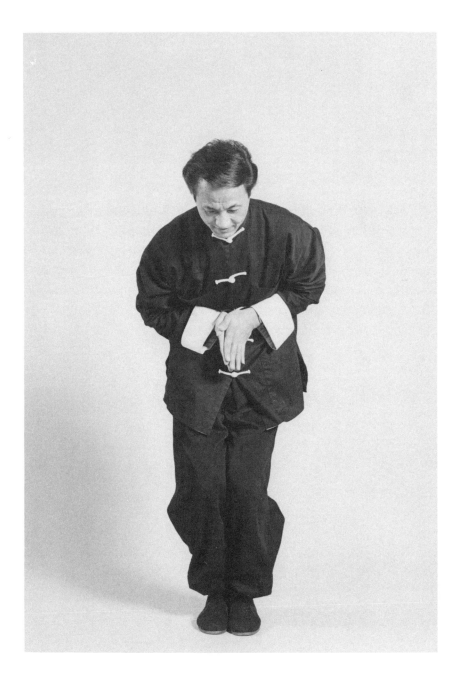

*figure 29*

Now move your two hands, palms still joined together, across your solar plexus towards the right. Turn your head and hips to the left. Your center of gravity continues to rise, and your knees continue to unbend. As your hands come to your right side they turn over, your left palm pressing your right. At the same time your hips should swing towards the left.

*figure 30*

77

Your hands now turn over as they continue to move upward once again. Your right hand is now on top of your left, fingers pointing to the left.

*figure 31*

Your hands now move to the left beneath your chin as your head turns to the front.

*figure 32*

81

Continue moving your two hands towards your left and begin aiming your finger tips upwards, starting a semicircular movement around the side of your head and past the top. At the same time, swing your hips to the right and then back towards the center, returning your head to the forward position.

*figure* 33

83

*figure 34*

*figure 35*

You are now in a full standing position, and your hands are palm to palm directly over your head with your arms inclining forwards slightly.

*figure 36*

*figure* 37

87

Shift the weight to the balls of the feet. The heels of both feet are raised up as your arms become fully extended, so that you are standing on your toes and your buttocks are held tightly together. Stretch up without straining while maintaining your balance on the balls of your feet and toes.

*figure 38*

*figure 39*

Hold this position for a few seconds. Slowly lower your hands, still joined palm to palm, in front of your face until they are beneath your chin in prayer position. As you do so, lower your heels.

*figure 40*

Now bring your hands down to rest over your lower tan-t'ien. Both palms now face tan-t'ien with the first two fingers of one hand touching the first two fingers of the other and thumb touching thumb, forming an inverted triangle.

The lao-kung points, in the middle of the palms (*see figure 41*), face the tan-t'ien and are quietly placed there until breathing becomes normal—about 30-45 seconds. During this time keep your mind focused in your palms and in your lower tan-t'ien. If you can, feel that the energy in the centers of your palms is communicating with the energy in your tan-t'ien. If you do not feel this at the outset, do not worry. As your Swimming Dragon practice develops, you will feel a flow of warmth in both your palms and your tan-t'ien.

After your breathing and heartbeat slow down to normal, repeat the exercise. After twenty minutes of practice, finish by slowly relaxing your two hands and bringing them down to the sides of your thighs.

*figure 41*

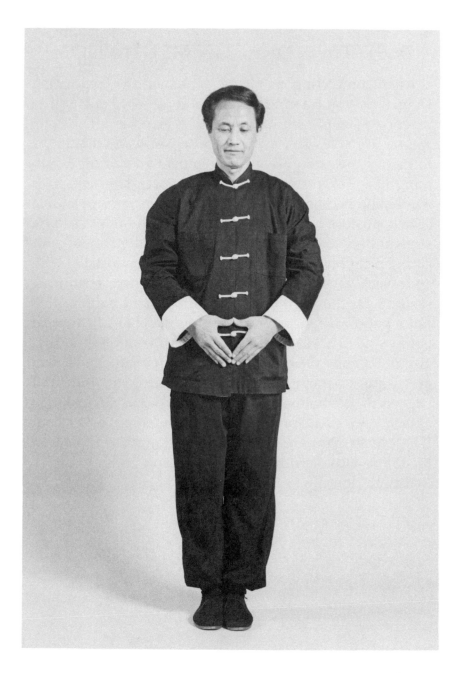

*figure 42*

# 3: SITTING DRAGON MEDITATION

After completing as many cycles of the Swimming Dragon as you intend to practice, it is very beneficial to practice a simple sitting meditation exercise for as long as you are able. The main purpose of this meditation is to gather the energy you have generated during Swimming Dragon and store it in your lower tan-t'ien. This meditation is called "Sitting Dragon." It is performed in a seated posture, either cross-legged on the floor or on a straight back chair. The most important thing about your sitting position is that you be able to sit comfortably with your back erect. For many people the best posture is seated near the front of a chair with a hard bottom. It is not a good idea to practice in a lounge chair. If the seat is too soft it is very difficult to sit up comfortably. It is also not a good idea to lean back on the seat, even if you are using a straight-backed chair. Sitting on the front edge of a flat-bottomed, straight-backed chair makes it easy to keep your spine vertical without strain or tension. If, however, you are practiced at sitting cross-legged on the floor, with or without a cushion, and prefer to do so, that is all right.

*figure 43*

95

To begin, place your hands in the position given in the illustration. To do this, place the tip of the thumb of your right hand at the base of the inside of the ring finger of your left hand. Next place the inner tip of the middle finger of your right hand at the base of the outside of the ring finger of your left hand. Finally, bring the tip of the thumb of your left hand to touch the tip of the middle finger of your left hand. Allow the remaining fingers of your right hand to touch the backs of the fingers of your left hand, and place both hands in front of your lower tan-t'ien.

*figure 44*

Major meridians run through your hands and terminate at your finger tips. This position allows the ch'i flowing through several of these meridians to circulate in a very beneficial way.

Now make sure your spine is comfortably vertical. The spine should be in the same condition as during the opening of the Swimming Dragon form: your head should feel suspended from the pai-hui point, floating upward as if on its own. Your spine should be fully extended. If you pay close attention to your spine, you should be able to feel that each vertebra is aligned above and below its neighbors. Your body weight should be released downward.

*figure 45*

Bring your mind, that is your attention, to your lower tan-t'ien. Let yourself breathe naturally and deeply. You should be able to feel, on each inhalation, your lower abdomen expanding gently. Feel that you are breathing into your tan-t'ien. When your breathing is deep in this way, you may also feel that the area in your back directly behind your tan-t'ien is also expanding gently. Do not force air into the lower part of your lungs. Simply allow yourself to breathe naturally and deeply, and notice the movement of your abdomen as you breathe.

You may close your eyes if you wish, or, if you keep your eyes open, they should not be focused on anything external, but rather it should be as if you were looking inward to your tan-t'ien.

Simply sit in this position, with your mind on your tan-t'ien, as long as you are able.

## Common Experiences During Practice

Once you have mastered the method of performing the Swimming Dragon to the point where your body is relaxed and your mind free from worrying about what to do next, you soon have experiences indicating that your internal ch'i energy is beginning to "move." These experiences come in many forms—different people experience ch'i in different ways. Typically you may begin to feel an internal warmth—an actual feeling of heat—along the limbs, within the lower tan-t'ien, and in the palms of your hands. Many people find that, as their practice develops, they feel more and more deeply relaxed with each cycle of the movement. Some people feel sensations of tingling and lightness, others experience a sensation of swelling or buoyancy within their body. Also you may notice that the atmosphere around your body seems to be growing warmer, or that it appears to be of a slightly thicker substance than normal, as if, during practice, your body were moving through water rather than air. These experiences or others like them will come and go as your practice develops. Notice them and enjoy them. They are signs that the exercise is working.

There is another kind of experience that is quite common during the first few months of practice; it does not have to do with the movement of ch'i, but rather with the loosening and realignment of bones and joints that the Swimming Dragon allows to occur. You may hear and feel distinct crackings or poppings of joints and bones deep inside your arms, shoulders, and back—somewhat like cracking your knuckles. The Swimming Dragon moves joints and muscles that are seldom, if ever, used in our daily activities. The cracking and opening of the joints give some people a sensation of release, much like a chiropractic adjustment.

## Additional Pointers

### The "S" Curve

When practicing Swimming Dragon, the spine is pulled open to its maximum limit and makes an "S" shape, with each joint of the head, neck, and spine moving together in the form of a "swimming dragon." As the "S" curve appears, all the vertebrae are gently stretched apart and a pleasurable sensation of release and space within the spine will occur. As in chiropractic, this stretching of the spine aids the free flow of lactic acid, reducing general fatigue.

### Think of the Blossoming of Youth

When first standing and preparing to practice (before each individual round) your entire body should be relaxed and quiet. Your attention should be focused on the middle of your palms. When your palms are joined together, begin to think of youthfulness and the blossoming of the prime of life. This mental guidance arouses the central nervous system and is helpful for relaxing the body. When you are in good spirits and the practice is performed with enthusiasm, the self-restoring functions of the human body are strengthened.

## Joining the Palms

Your palms are joined together throughout the entire exercise (*see figure 46*). This integrates the yin and yang so that no ch'i escapes out of the body. The palms and fingers should remain in constant contact, but the hands should not become stiff or tense. The fingers remain together and should not fan apart.

*figure 46*

## "Shaking the Tail"

When your hands swing to one side, your buttocks swing as far as they can go in the opposite direction. This movement, called "shaking the tail," is unbroken and continuous, again like the movement of a swimming dragon. "Shaking the tail" is the key to the movement of the tendons and bones. As these movements are performed by the waist and abdomen, this promotes the "burning" of fat that has accumulated in these areas.

## Gentle Contraction of the Groin Area

Your heels are placed next to each other and your thighs are squeezed together during the entire cycle of the Swimming Dragon. This produces physiological effects during the movements which regulate internal secretions. Most of the fat of middle aged and older people is accumulated due to functional reduction of the secretions of internal organs and glandular hormones, together with the lowering of basal metabolism. Practice of this exercise has marked effects in dealing with these problems.

## Raising the heels

Swimming Dragon is dominated by the waist. The movement is manifested in the head and the power issues forth from the legs. This causes the ch'i to circulate within the body and not to flow out of it. This "holding" of ch'i constitutes a major feature of traditional Taoist exercises. The raising and lowering of the center of weight and the raising of the heels (at the end of each round) can arouse the three yin channels and three yang channels that terminate in the feet. This also has effects on the liver, spleen, and kidney channels. At the same time, raising the heels pulls and stretches the body to its maximum limit and causes the buttocks and abdomen to contract.

### How to Find the Pai-hui Point

Throughout the Swimming Dragon and Relaxed Standing Forms, your body should feel as if it were suspended from a point at the top of your head, called the pai-hui point.

Pai-hui is located at the crown of the head, and can be found in the following way: at the base of your skull on the back of the head are the ends of two prominent bones (called the occipital condyles). Between these two bones is a "dip" or "valley." Place the thumb of your right hand in this valley and lay your palm over your cranium (skull) so that your right pinky extends towards the crown of your head. Now place the pinky of your left hand on the bridge of your nose between your eyes. Lay the palm of your left hand over your forehead so that your left thumb reaches towards the crown of your head. Very close to where the thumb of your left hand and the pinky of your right hand meet, there is a slight indentation in your cranium. In this indentation is your pai-hui point.

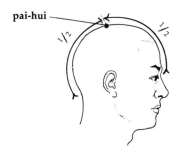

*figure 47*

Throughout the form you should feel as if your head were being suspended from the sky at this point. It is as if your head were a helium balloon—as if there were something in your head that were naturally tending to lift it gently but definitely off the spine and towards the sky through the pai-hui point. This feeling of your head being gently lifted off your spine is something that you need to discover for yourself as you practice the form. It is not something that you should force to happen by stiffly pushing your head up. There actually is a way for your head to float very naturally up off the top of your spine, but it happens more as a result of your imagining it rising up with your mind than by your moving it upward by muscular effort.

When you do discover how to let your head float up off your spine through the pai-hui point towards the sky, you will find that this discovery also allows your spine to relax and at the same time releases all the weight of your body so that it sinks down naturally. When you feel this sinking, you should direct your weight to the kidney points at the bottom of your feet (*see next section*). It will feel as if your whole body were being suspended from above with all your weight sinking down through your legs and feet and into the ground.

## Weight on Kidney Points

Throughout the Swimming Dragon exercise your weight should remain centered over your two kidney points on the bottoms of your feet. These points are the acupuncture points that are located at the end of the meridian associated with the kidney. The Chinese name for the kidney point, (Yung Ch'uan), means "bubbling well," because when your weight is evenly centered over your kidney points it is as if ch'i energy were bubbling up from the ground and entering your body. This bubbling up of energy can actually be experienced during Swimming Dragon practice and during standing meditation.

*figure 48*

105

The kidney point is located in the center of the foot just behind the "ball" in the soft area that corresponds to the palm of the hand (*see figure 49*). It is a good idea to locate the kidney point manually while sitting down. It is usually somewhat sensitive to pressure. Massaging the kidney point can be very soothing and beneficial to the whole body. As a matter of fact, one feature of the Swimming Dragon is that each cycle uses the weight of the body to perform such a massage.

When you are practicing Swimming Dragon, the weight of your body should remain focused evenly on the kidney points of your two feet. As your weight will naturally tend to shift a little bit to the left, right, front, and back as you perform the movement, there will be a tendency to shift your weight from foot to foot. This tendency should be countered by trying to keep your weight evenly distributed. A little bit of movement should be tolerated, however, as this movement massages the points.

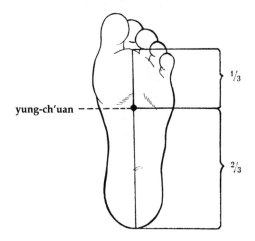

*figure 49*

## Advanced Breathing

After you have mastered the Swimming Dragon form and have been practicing it regularly for a month, you can add the following breathing instructions:

As you begin the form, while your joined palms are rising toward your chin, begin a long and slow inhalation. Continue inhaling as your hands circle your head and until they have passed beneath your chin. At this point begin to exhale slowly. Your exhalation should be timed to continue throughout the downward movement of the Swimming Dragon. When you have reached the lowest point and are about to begin your bottom-to-top movement, begin to inhale. This inhalation should last until you have completed the bottom-to-top movement, with your arms fully extended above your head. While you are standing in this position on the balls and toes of your feet, you should hold your breath, feeling your lungs expanded to the maximum. When you begin to come down from this position, begin your exhalation. As your hands take their place in front of your lower tan-t'ien, return to natural breathing.

# Related Taoist Practices

## Taoist Relaxation Meditation

The following practice is a general exercise for relaxing your muscles, nerves, and organs. Perhaps a few words are necessary about what it means to "relax your organs." In Chinese medicine each organ is associated with a meridian or channel that runs either from or to the organ, along the arms, legs, or trunk. The name of an organ refers not only to—for instance—the heart, liver, or kidney, but to the entire internal system of which the organ itself is a part. The organ/meridian system as a whole can be affected by the kind of attention we pay to it. When we allow ourselves to pay attention to an organ with a happy, relaxed and peaceful attitude, we can actually help that organ to function peacefully and strongly. Now, each organ has a characteristic internal feeling that you can learn to sense as you develop your practice. When you are instructed to relax your liver, for instance, what you do is bring your attention to the area in your body occupied by your liver, sense its characteristic internal feeling, and imagine the liver area becoming peaceful and serene. Before you become familiar with the characteristic feeling, simply bring your attention to the area in your body where the organ is located, while being attentive to any sensations you are aware of in that area and let go of any tension you feel there. If you do this practice frequently, you will soon become familiar with the characteristic sensations of each organ and you will develop your ability to help your organs "relax."

Taoist Relaxation Meditation is performed in a seated posture, either cross-legged on the floor or on a straight back chair. The instructions for the sitting position are the same as for "Sitting Dragon" given above (*see page 94*). The only difference is what you do with your hands: place your hands palm down on your thighs, about half way between your hips and your knees. Turn your hands inward very slightly; that is, let your middle fingers point inward. This will open up the area under the shoulders by keeping your upper arms from resting against your sides.

Sit with your spine erect and balanced but not rigid or tense. All the vertebrae should line up on top of each other nicely. Feel as if there were an ever increasing distance between each of your vertebrae, as if your spine were growing ever so slightly taller, moment by moment.

Feel that your whole body is relaxed and suspended from above at the pai-hui point (*see 'Additional Pointers,' page 103*). Feel as though your head has a tendency to float upward directly through that point. It is as if your head is a lighter-than-air helium balloon—a balloon that rises vertically entirely on its own without being pulled or pushed.

Throughout this exercise, breathe quietly and naturally through your mouth. Keep your teeth lightly together, and allow the tip of the tongue to gently touch the roof of your mouth.

Throughout the exercise allow your breathing to reach deeply into your lower abdomen to your lower tan-t'ien (*see page 11*). Relax your tan-t'ien and allow your inhalations to gently expand. Your ch'i will thereby accumulate in your tan-t'ien. If you practice Taoist Relaxation Meditation and Swimming Dragon regularly, you will be able to feel the ch'i accumulating there.

In the following meditation exercise you progressively relax your body, giving your body the gentle suggestion to relax, part by part. The exercise is performed by going through four cycles of suggestion, each cycle beginning at the top of the head and moving down your body.

## *First Cycle*

Begin by bringing your attention to the top of your head as you inhale, consciously relaxing your scalp as you exhale.

With your next inhalation, bring your attention to the sides of your head, relaxing the sides of your head as you exhale.

With your next breath, bring your attention to the sides of your neck and shoulders and relax them as you exhale. Notice if there is any tension in your neck and shoulders. Breathe slowly three or four more times, relaxing as you exhale.

Proceed in a similar manner, moving your attention as you inhale and giving the suggestion to relax as you exhale, through the following parts of your body in the order given:

> shoulders
> arms

110

wrists (it helps to relax the small-finger side of wrist)

fingers

Complete the first cycle by bring your attention to your middle fingers and breathing three times, relaxing on the exhalation.

## Second Cycle

Bring your attention once again to the top of your head and relax each of the following bodily parts, moving attention on to your inhalation and giving the suggestion to relax on exhalation:

top of head
eyebrows
between eyes
sides of nose
mouth
face
front of neck
front of chest
belly
crotch
knees
ankles
toes

Complete the second cycle by bringing your attention to your big toes and giving suggestion to relax while exhaling three times.

## Third Cycle

Bring your attention once again to the top of your head and relax each of the following bodily parts, moving attention on your inhalation and giving the suggestion to relax on exhalation:

> top of head
> back of head
> back of neck
> upper back
> lower back
> hips
> backs of knees
> heels

Complete the third cycle by bringing your attention to your kidney points (these are located at the center of the feet—*see diagram*) and giving suggestion to relax while exhaling three times.

## Fourth Cycle

Bring your attention once again to the top of your head and relax each of the following bodily parts, moving attention on your inhalation and giving the suggestion to relax on exhalation:

> top of head
> eyes (feel that your eyes are smiling as you look
>     within)
> center of head behind eyes
> lungs
> kidneys
> liver

heart
spleen
stomach
tan-t'ien (energy field 3 fingers below navel)

To complete the relaxation meditation, place your palms over your lower tan-t'ien. Women should place their right palm on the inside, left palm outside; men should place their left palm on the inside, right palm outside.

With your hands in this position, gently massage the area in front of your tan-t'ien.

First, make 36 circles. Begin with very small circles and gradually increase their radius. Women should make these circles in a counterclockwise direction (down the right side, up the left side), men in a clockwise direction (down the left side, up the right side).

When you have completed these 36 expanding circles, make 24 circles in the opposite direction (women clockwise, men counterclockwise) beginning with circles of a wide radius, and contracting them slowly as you proceed.

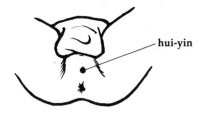

*figure 50*

## Standing Meditation:
## The Relaxed and Calm Standing Form

In addition to sitting meditation and relaxation practices, Taoist ch'i kung exercises include meditations that are performed while standing. Standing meditation practice is a very effective way of encouraging the production and storage of ch'i. The basic meditation is called the "Relaxed and Calm Standing Form." It is performed without movement for as long as one desires. It is good to practice this form for a few minutes before practicing The Swimming Dragon, but The Relaxed and Calm Standing Form can also be developed as a practice in its own right.

To develop the Relaxed and Calm Standing Form, begin with a few minutes practice each day and gradually increase the length of time of practice until you can stand without discomfort for at least a half hour.

The "Relaxed And Calm Standing Form" consists of eighteen specific requirements:

1. stand with feet parallel at shoulder-width
2. bend your knees
3. relax your hips
4. round your crotch
5. gently contract your anus
6. contract your abdomen
7. relax your waist
8. sink your chest without collapsing it
9. raise your back but don't hunch it
10. allow your shoulders to hang down
11. drop your elbows
12. open your armpits

13. relax your wrists
14. think that your head is suspended from above
15. pull in your chin slightly
16. close your eyes gently
17. close your lips
18. place your tongue against your upper palate

## 1. Stand with feet parallel at shoulder-width

For position of feet, see figure 6. Allow your body weight to sink to the bottom of your feet, distributed evenly between them. You should feel your weight sink down into the ground through the yung-ch'uan points (*see page 106*). This lays the foundation for relaxing the waist (requirement 7). A wider stance is permissible together with a deeper bend at the knees as your practice develops. It is also permissible to point your feet slightly outward or inward if this is more comfortable.

## 2. Bend your knees

Allow your knees to bend as far as they can comfortably. Generally, the further your knees can bend the more ch'i you will generate. Do not force yourself to bend your knees further than they "want" to go—as your practice develops, you will naturally bend them further. The knee joints are important for circulating ch'i and blood to the feet. When your knees are relaxed and not stiff and straight, the ch'i and blood can flow freely. This helps relax the hips (requirement 3), round the crotch (requirement 4), and relax the waist (requirement 7).

### 3. Relax your hips
Relax the joints of the hipbones.

### 4. Round your crotch
The crotch is "rounded" in three steps. First, make sure your knees are bent and not held tense; second, let the knees move slightly outward without forcing; third, allow the crotch to hang so as to raise the hui-yin point (*see figure 50*) and slightly raise the anus.

Placing the knees correctly must be integrated with relaxing the joints of the hipbones. When the hipbones are relaxed and the hips are raised, the knees naturally will tend to be in the right position, making the lower extremities light and flexible.

The knees should be held at maximum distance apart from each other, preventing any "caving in" of the legs towards each other. At the same time the hip joints are drawn back as far as possible, without allowing the trunk of the body to tilt forward. There is a two-fold opening in the area of the sacrum—the muscles around the sacrum are expanded both vertically and horizontally and at the same time opened and relaxed. The sacrum itself should be held erect, with the coccyx alone tucked forward, sending the weight of the body into the legs. The spine should rest vertically above the sacrum, without either leaning backward or tilting forward.

This whole aspect of the standing form is called "rounding the crotch." Rounding the crotch makes it so that the hui-yin point is neither too open or too constricted. Non-constriction of the hui-yin allows a free flow of ch'i. Not opening it too widely prevents the ch'i from flowing out.

116

## 5. Gently contract your anus

This is performed mentally—think that your anus is contracted very gently and imagine that it is being slightly drawn up into your body.

## 6. Contract your abdomen

Contract slightly your lower abdomen above the pubic bones, but do not strain the muscles of the abdominal region. Contracting the abdomen can help to collect ch'i in the tan-t'ien and promote circulation of ch'i throughout the body.

## 7. Relax your waist

If the waist is not relaxed, the ch'i cannot sink to the tan-t'ien. The basis of relaxing the waist is relaxing the hips and bending the knees. Relaxing the waist will also make the vertebrae erect and enable them to "relax down." A good method for relaxing the waist is as follows: raise your shoulders up and then immediately release them. Then exhale deeply one time. Relaxing the waist is the key to relaxation in general and can also help to make the sacrum more flexible. The sacrum has a "false" joint which most people are unable to move, with the exception of women during pregnancy. Those who practice ch'i kung regularly are able to open the "false" joint of the sacrum allowing the tan-t'ien to expand and accumulate ch'i for future use.

## 8. Sink your chest without collapsing it

To "sink" the chest, make it "empty," that is, don't forcefully expand your chest military style—just let it relax. Do not forcefully pull in your shoulders. Allow the thoracic vertebrae to sink down and relax. (The thoracic vertebrae are the vertebrae in the middle region of the spine.) When these vertebrae are empty and sunken, the chest-rib area will open out and allow the chest area to relax. This will expand the chest area naturally without straining the chest muscles.

### 9. Raise your back but don't hunch it

The key to raising the back without hunching it lies in letting the shoulders hang down (requirement 10). When the shoulders are even and hanging, the waist joints will also be straight.

The function of sinking the chest and raising the back is to ease pressure on the heart and lungs. Easing pressure on the heart improves one's "spirit" since in traditional Chinese medicine the heart governs not only the circulation of the blood but the spirit. When the thoracic cavity is open and the spine is straight, the mind becomes calm and tranquil and the lobes of the lungs grow clear and resounding. Sinking the chest and raising the back, by relaxing them both, also enhances circulation of ch'i through the ren and du channels.

### 10. Allow your shoulders to hang down.

Relax your shoulder joints and let them hang naturally. This promotes the relaxation not only of the shoulders themselves, but the back and neck.

### 11. Drop your elbows

Bend your elbows slightly and then let them drop down. Your mind should be focused on the tips of your elbows and they should feel light and free as if they were suspended in midair. They should be tipped slightly outward. Your arms should hang down by your sides, palms facing your thighs.

### 12. Open your armpits
The key to both opening your armpits and letting your shoulders hang is letting your elbows tip outward slightly. Be careful not to let your shoulders slip forward or rise upward. When your armpits are opened, the ch'i and blood of the upper extremities can circulate freely.

### 13. Relax your wrists
Let your wrists be loose and relaxed, with the palms of your hands facing your thighs. Let the fingers of each hand touch each other loosely, neither extending them stiffly nor allowing them to curl or bend limply.

Relaxing the wrists allows circulation between shoulders and fingers to flow freely, while keeping the fingers naturally extended and the palms facing the thighs prevents ch'i from flowing out.

### 14. Think that your head is suspended from above
Let your head be centered comfortably on top of your spine as if it were suspended from above the pai-hui point (*see page 103*).

Bring your attention to this point and relax your scalp. Your head should feel light and empty, and be able to move nimbly on your spine. When the head moves in this condition the entire body will feel centered and it will be able to maintain its upright position easily. Bringing your attention to the top of your scalp while your whole body is relaxed, centered and erect, naturally guides the ch'i upward to cultivate the brain, nourish the mind, and enhance the activities of the entire body.

### 15. Pull in your chin slightly

Without tilting your head forward, draw in your lower jaw. When you draw the lower jaw in, it is easy to feel that your whole head is being suspended from above the pai-hui point. This also allows free and smooth breathing. This also opens the channels in the back of the neck allowing ch'i to flow freely to and from the head.

### 16. Close your eyes gently

Let your eyelids cover your eyes lightly as if they were falling curtains. Let your upper eyelids fall naturally but do not close your eyes tightly. When the eyelids are lightly closed, spirit is held within, spirit and mind are calmed.

### 17. Close your lips

Let your lips close lightly, but close your teeth by letting your molars bite together. This is a method for raising yang energy. Bringing the lips together prevents the ch'i from flowing out.

### 18. Place your tongue against your upper palate

Let the tongue adhere to the palate in back of the upper teeth without force. The tongue acts as a bridge over which ch'i can cross between the ren and du channels (*see page 121*). Also when the tongue touches the upper palate the amount of saliva increases. Saliva contains many types of enzymes which not only aid digestion but, according to Chinese medicine, benefit one's physiology in other ways.

Stand in this position with your hands facing your thighs until you are relaxed and comfortable. Then bring your attention to your hands and arms and allow your hands to rise slowly until they are approximately at the level of your middle tan-t'ien. Your fingers should be extended but not stretched or tense. They should be pointing towards each other, first finger of right hand pointing to first finger of left, and so on. Your palms should be facing your body. As you develop this practice you will be able to feel the presence of a ball of ch'i energy enclosed by your arms and upper torso. Actually the ball is formed by a circle that extends all the way around your back. In order to feel the energy ball, your shoulders must be free and open. There should be a slight space under your shoulders, between the upper part of your under arms and the upper part of your sides.

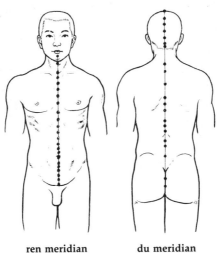

ren meridian      du meridian

*figure 51*

121

Do not lift your elbows, but simply allow your hands to rise into position (*see figure 52*). When the eighteen points are performed correctly, it should be possible to remain in this position for as long as you wish without your arms becoming fatigued.

## About Master Shih

Tzu Kuo Shih was born in 1929 in Shanghai, the third son of Ding Wen Shih, a Chinese Doctor who represented the fifth generation of a family of famous practitioners of Chinese medicine.

Master Shih began his study of ch'i kung at the age of eleven. At this time he was suffering from T.B. and malaria contracted after the Japanese bombing of Shanghai, during which he lost his father and uncle. His grandfather taught him a special Buddhist ch'i kung form and cured him.

Master Shih continued to study ch'i kung throughout his youth under the instruction of various famous Buddhist and Taoist masters. At the same time, while living with his father's brother (another well-known doctor practicing traditional Chinese medicine) he learned acupuncture, including a special technique of head-acupuncture that had been developed by his ancestors and perfected by his famous grandfather.

Master Shih began his own medical career in 1949 as an assistant to the celebrated Dr. Yzi Wing Bei. While still in his twenties he began his life-long association with the Taoist traditions of Wu Tang Mountain, the traditional birthplace of Chinese martial arts. From Pan Tzu Shih Yea and his son, Pan Ch'un, he learned the secret Wu Tang form of tai chi chuan. In the 1970s, Dr. Shih and Dr. Bei were allowed to publish their books on Wu Tang t'ai chi, making most of this form public.

Dr. Shih is a recognized Master of three other styles of t'ai chi, in addition to Wu Tang : Wu, Sun and Yang. Among the masters from whom he studied the Yang style was Po Pin Ju, one of the legendary Yang Chen Fu's "ten special students."

Besides his accomplishments as a physician and Master of ch'i kung and the martial arts, Master Shih is also an excellent calligrapher and a fine painter in several traditional Chinese styles. He is currently living, practicing and teaching in Kingston, New York where he directs the Chinese Healing Arts Center and the Wu Tang Chuan Kung Association and publishes the Wu Tang Chuan Kung Newsletter, dedicated to the dissemination of information about traditional Chinese healing practices.

Tzu Kuo Shih is acknowledged as one of China's leading experts in ch'i kung; he is a recognized Master of four styles of t'ai chi chuan. He has authored books on Pa Kua Ch'i Kung and Wu Tang Ch'i Kung, as well as standard articles on Wu Tang T'ai Chi, and other works on chinese medicine and martial arts. He is an Honorary Director of the China Ch'i Kung Research Association, and consultant to the Wu Tang Chuan Research Association and the Ch'i Kung Research Association of Shanghai. He is a lecturer at the Shanghai College of Traditional Chinese Medicine and Senior Consultant to the Hoping Bio-Medical Technology Research Institute.